EXPLORE COLONIAL AMERICA

THE SALEM WITCH TRIALS

Sarah Gilman

Enslow Publishing
101 W. 23rd Street
Suite 240
New York, NY 10011
USA

enslow.com

Published in 2017 by Enslow Publishing, LLC.
101 W. 23rd Street, Suite 240, New York, NY 10011

Library of Congress Cataloging-in-Publication Data

Names: Gilman, Sarah, author.
Title: The Salem witch trials / Sarah Gilman.
Description: New York, NY : Enslow Publishing, 2017. |Series title: Exploring Colonial America | Includes bibliographical references and index.
Identifiers: LCCN 2015050573| ISBN 9780766078741 (library bound) | ISBN 9780766078802 (pbk.) | ISBN 9780766078628 (6-pack)
Subjects: LCSH: Trials (Witchcraft)--Massachusetts--Salem--Juvenile literature. | Witchcraft--Massachusetts--Salem--History--Juvenile literature.
Classification: LCC KFM2478.8.W5 G55 2016 | DDC 345.744/50288--dc23
LC record available at http://lccn.loc.gov/2015050573

To Our Readers: We have done our best to make sure all website addresses in this book were active and appropriate when we went to press. However, the author and the publisher have no control over and assume no liability for the material available on those websites or on any websites they may link to. Any comments or suggestions can be sent by e-mail to customerservice@enslow.com.

Portions of this book originally appeared in the book *Witness the Salem Witchcraft Trials* by Elaine Landau.

CONTENTS

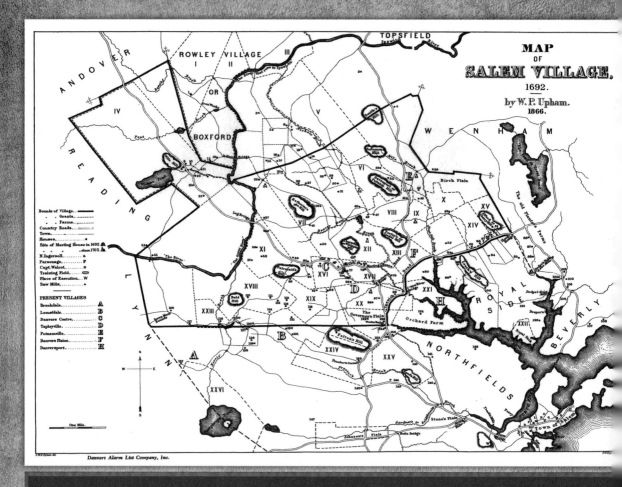

During the late seventeenth century, the sleepy village of Salem, Massachusetts, was the setting of a particularly odd turn of events. Baseless accusations resulted in the death of many citizens.

CHAPTER
ONE

CURIOUS BEHAVIOR

During the long, cold winter of 1691, blizzards had struck Massachusetts for weeks. The heavy snows and freezing winds made it hard to be outdoors.

The young people of Salem Village were stuck inside. This was especially true for the girls. Unlike the boys, they did not even leave the house to hunt for animals. There was little for them to do. Often they felt lonely and bored.

Salem Village could be a lonely place in any case. It was miles from the town of Salem, which was a trade center. Salem Village was mostly made up of farms. There was a meetinghouse for religious services and not much else. Even these buildings were cold and uncomfortable during the winter. There never seemed to be enough firewood.

THE PARRIS HOUSE

Things were a bit better at the home of the village minister, Samuel Parris. His nine-year-old daughter, Betty, had her eleven-year-old cousin, Abigail, for company. Abigail Williams was an orphan who lived with the Parris family. She earned her keep by helping with household chores.

The girls also had Tituba. Tituba was one of the reverend's slaves. She had come from the island of Barbados in the Caribbean Sea, south of the United States we know today. Samuel Parris and his family had lived there for a time before coming to Salem Village. When he left the island, he brought a few slaves back with him. Tituba told the girls stories about magic spells and powerful spirits. People often did such things in Barbados, but not in Salem Village.

Sometimes, young women from the village visited Betty and Abigail. Among these were twelve-year-old Ann Putnam and seventeen-year-old Elizabeth Hubbard. At times, nineteen-year-old Mercy Lewis and sixteen-year-old Mary Wolcott came. There were others, too.

Many people believe that the young women begged Tituba to teach them fortune-telling games. Tituba may have told the girls to drop an egg white into a glass of water. The egg white would form a shape in a glass. The shape was supposed to be a sign of things to come.

EXPLORE THE FACTS

REVEREND PARRIS

Samuel Parris was not well-liked by everyone in Salem Village. Before agreeing to be minister, he insisted on a high salary and the deed to the house he was to live in.

Tituba was a slave from the islands. Her customs were different from those shared by the Parris family and the rest of Salem Village. She was easy to accuse of witchcraft.

DANGEROUS WITCHCRAFT

This had to be done in secret. The people of Salem Village were Puritans. They believed in living strictly by the Bible. The Puritans felt that a person's life should be filled with hard work and prayer. Anything else invited the devil into their lives.

Reverend Parris insisted on strict religious teaching for Betty and Abigail. He led them in prayer every day. On Sundays, they spent hours in church listening to his sermons and singing hymns.

The Puritans wanted nothing to do with what they thought were spells or witchcraft. Witchcraft was both a sin and a crime in Salem Village. In some cases, it was punishable by death.

This fear of witchcraft was not new to the Puritans. The Puritans came from Europe where witchcraft trials were common in both Germany and England. Between 1560 and 1760, nearly one hundred thousand people were found guilty of witchcraft there.

In New England, the Puritans wanted to be rid of witches as well. As early as 1648, a woman in the Massachusetts Colony had been hanged for witchcraft.

Asking Tituba to speak of magic spells and fortune-telling was dangerous. Yet somehow that did not seem to matter to the girls that winter. After all, these were just some silly young people at play. Surely, no real harm could come from this—or could it?

BEWITCHED!

In the middle of that bitter winter, in January 1692, Betty Parris started to act strangely. She was not hungry. Some days she would

In Europe in the middle ages, many women were burned at the stake for supposedly being witches. The religious people of Salem were always on the lookout for signs of the devil.

be forgetful or burst out crying. There were also times when Betty felt as though she was on fire.

At about the same time, Betty's cousin Abigail changed, too. She would fall to the floor and shake. Sometimes she would just babble. It was as if she were speaking in a strange language.

The village doctor, William Griggs, was called. He examined the girls and found nothing physically wrong with either of them. At the time, people did not know about mental illness, or problems people have with the way they think and behave. Therefore, Griggs felt that they must have been bewitched.

The girls did not get any better. Instead, the unusual behavior spread. By mid-February, their friends began acting the same way. Now Ann Putnam, Elizabeth Hubbard, Mercy Lewis, Mary Wolcott, and others were thought to be bewitched, too.

The villagers were upset. They wanted to know who had done this. Who was the witch among them?

Once Betty Parris became "bewitched," many of her friends became similarly hysterical. This scene from the movie *The Crucible* (1996) dramatizes the girls' behavior.

THE ACCUSATIONS BEGIN

Reverend Parris certainly did not want Satan, or the devil, in Salem Village. He especially did not want him near his own household. He became upset that the girls would not tell who had bewitched them.

Reverend Parris urged the girls to give names. Finally, Betty said that Tituba had bewitched them. The girls also named two other women in Salem Village. These were Sarah Osborne and Sarah Good. They were women who the girls knew were not well-liked by the villagers.

EASY MARKS

The three women named were likely choices. They were not very powerful. No one was going to come to their defense.

Reverend Samuel Parris was a powerful figure in Salem Village. He involved himself in many disputes among villagers and even framed one, Charles Stevens (above), for murder.

EXPLORE THE FACTS

POWERFUL WITCHCRAFT

The witch hunt made people think about their own lives. If a fence blew down in a storm before, they thought it was just bad luck. Now they were sure it was witchcraft.

Sarah Osborne was an elderly woman. Her many health problems often kept her at home. She had not set foot in church for over a year. This was a sin among the Puritans.

Few people liked Sarah Good. She was a poor, homeless woman. Sarah Good often begged for food. Sometimes people gave her nothing. Then she would walk angrily away. She muttered things no one understood. Perhaps they thought that she had put a curse on them.

Tituba was a slave woman with no rights. She was at the mercy of Reverend Parris, who often beat her. At times, Tituba would say anything to avoid a whipping.

These women had not done spells together. They may not have even known one another. However, that did not change things. On February 29, 1692, all three women were arrested.

As time wore on, more and more villagers—mostly women—were arrested for witchcraft. It seemed no one was safe, particularly those who were different or who had angered the Parris family for any reason.

CHAPTER THREE

QUESTIONING AT THE MEETINGHOUSE

Sarah Osborne, Sarah Good, and Tituba were questioned at the Salem Village meetinghouse on March 1. The room was packed with people. Everyone was anxious to see the accused.

They came to see the bewitched young women, too. Weeks had passed and the young women had not gotten any better. Reverend Parris prayed for them every day. He asked the members of his church to pray for them as well. When the young women did not improve, Parris ask other reverends from other towns to come to his home to pray. Yet, nothing helped those who seemed to be bewitched.

As this scene from a stage production of *The Crucible* (1953) suggests, those accused of witchcraft had little chance once put on trial.

THE WOMEN SPEAK

Two businessmen, Jonathan Corwin and John Hathorne, questioned the accused women. Neither had any legal training, but this was not unusual. Law in Salem Village was based on the Bible. These men had studied that book well. Many respected men in the community would be appointed magistrates or judges when the actual trials began.

Both Sarah Osborne and Sarah Good claimed to be innocent. The bewitched young women showed that they felt differently. They would grunt, groan, and scream out during the questioning.

Only the slave woman Tituba confessed to being a witch. She may have thought that Reverend Parris would beat her if she did not. Or perhaps she thought the judges would be easier on her if she confessed.

EXPLORE THE FACTS

A FAILED TEST

Sarah Good was asked to recite the Lord's Prayer to prove her innocence. Puritans believed that a witch couldn't do this. When she made a few mistakes, people were sure she was guilty.

TITUBA'S TESTIMONY

In any case, Tituba described a tall man dressed in black. Sometimes he had a yellow bird with him. He was supposed to be the devil. Tituba said that the man in black made her sign a book. She added that she had not been the only one from Salem Village to sign. Tituba said that four other women had signed and that Sarah Good and Sarah Osborne were among them. This was their pact or agreement with the devil.

Tituba told how the devil made her hurt the bewitched young women. She said that the devil would come to her in different forms. Sometimes, he looked like a hog, while other times he appeared as a large dog. Tituba said that she felt forced to do whatever he asked. She also spoke of frightening creatures such as huge red ants and talking cats.

The people believed Tituba. They thought that witches were real and feared their powers. They did not want to see evil at work in Salem Village.

After being questioned, the three accused women were taken to a jail in Boston. They would remain there until their actual trials.

But that did not end the trouble in Salem Village. It was just the start of things to come.

The women and men who were accused by the "bewitched" girls were made to await their trails in jail. To add insult to injury, they were forced to pay for their own imprisonment.

THE WITCH HUNT CONTINUES

With the three accused witches safely in jail, things should have gone back to normal in Salem Village. But the bewitched girls did not get better. The villagers prayed for help. They wondered if the devil was still at work. Were there more witches among them?

MARTHA COREY

The bewitched young women said there were. On March 11, Ann Putnam accused Martha Corey of witchcraft. Corey was not like the other accused women. She was a churchgoer, but she was known to speak her mind. This was unusual in a Puritan woman. Some in Salem Village felt that Corey did not know how women were supposed to behave.

Martha Corey was questioned at the meetinghouse on March 21. She swore that she was innocent. Yet the bewitched young women made that hard to believe. They twisted their bodies as if they were in terrible pain. They also copied every movement Corey made. Not surprisingly, Martha Corey was jailed.

REBECCA NURSE

Everyone was shocked when the next person, seventy-one-year-old Rebecca Nurse, was accused. Rebecca Nurse never missed church. She was also known for her goodness. Nevertheless, the bewitched young women insisted that she was a witch. When Nurse was questioned, some of the village people spoke up for her. They reminded the magistrates of Nurse's kindness to others. It did not help. Nurse was soon jailed with the others.

Soon, Nurse's sister Mary Easty was also arrested. Before this, Easty had never been accused of any wrongdoing. Now she was questioned and sent to jail to await trial.

LITTLE DORCAS GOOD

By the end of March, five people had been locked up for witchcraft. Among these was Sarah Good's five-year-old daughter, Dorcas. After she confessed to being a witch, Dorcas went to jail as well. No one knows why Dorcas confessed. She may have been scared. It is also likely that the small child just wanted to be with her mother. In April, Sarah Good gave birth to a baby in prison. The baby died a few weeks later.

Being jailed was not easy for young Dorcas. Despite her age, she was treated as harshly as an adult. When the jailer's iron chains

A faithful churchgoer, Martha Corey was accused of being a witch. Corey was known to be outspoken, and that was not considered a proper trait for women.

slipped off her hands, tiny iron handcuffs had to be made for her. The girl's family had to pay for these.

Women continued to be accused and jailed. Often, these were relatives of those already accused of witchcraft. Others had been in some sort of problem with one of the bewitched young women's families. Still others had openly doubted the bewitched young women's claims. Life was now very dangerous for many in Salem Village.

CHAPTER FIVE

THOSE WHO DIDN'T BELIEVE

There were some villagers who did not believe the girls were bewitched. Some of these people thought that the girls were "out of their wits" or insane. Others felt that they just wanted attention. Yet, few dared to question the young women. They feared that they might be accused of witchcraft as well.

THE PROCTORS

That was what happened to a sixty-year-old tavern owner named John Proctor. Proctor did not believe the young women were bewitched. He had even suggested that they "be had to the Whipping post." Proctor felt that the girls should be beaten rather than believed.

Anyone who doubted the girls was subject to accusation. John and Elizabeth Proctor were taken to jail when their own servant, whom they did not believe, pointed her finger at them.

Then his young servant girl, Mary Warren, started acting bewitched. After Proctor threatened to beat her if she did not stop, Mary calmed down. However, before long, the troublesome behavior began again. Now Mary accused John Proctor's wife of being a witch. She said that Elizabeth Proctor tried to make her sign the devil's book.

John Proctor went to his wife's hearing on April 11. He tried to defend her. Proctor insisted that his wife was innocent. This angered her accusers. During the hearing, the girls claimed that John Proctor was a wizard (a male witch) as well. The Proctors were taken to jail.

GEORGE BURROUGHS

Even ministers were being accused of witchcraft, like the Reverend George Burroughs. Though Burroughs used to be Salem Village's minister, he was now living in Maine.

Nevertheless, Ann Putnam accused him of being a wizard. On May 4, George Burroughs was arrested and brought to Salem Village for questioning. Burroughs doubted that he would be treated fairly in Salem Village. He knew that the judges did not like him. He had quarreled with some of them before leaving for Maine. Burroughs was right. He was soon jailed.

SPECTRAL EVIDENCE

As more people were accused, some began to question the idea of spectral evidence. This was the fact that a person could say in court that another person's spirit left his or her body and harmed others. No one could see these spirits except the bewitched young women.

Reverend George Burroughs stands in chains during his trial. Burroughs was brought back from Maine after Ann Putnam randomly accused him.

EXPLORE THE FACTS

BLAST FROM THE PAST

George Burroughs was very surprised when he was arrested for being a wizard. He had not seen his accuser, Ann Putnam, since she was a toddler.

That made it impossible for the accused, those people who were on trial, to defend themselves. Those accused could not prove that an invisible (unseen) spirit had not left their bodies.

The judges accepted spectral evidence, but not everyone in Salem Village was comfortable with this. This was especially true when respected members of the community were accused. Yet before long, many people would be found guilty on spectral evidence alone.

CHAPTER
SIX

THE ACCUSED GO ON TRIAL

By the time the trials began in mid-June, more than 150 of the 1,680 people living in Salem Village had been jailed for witchcraft. The nine trial judges were appointed by William Phips, the Massachusetts Colony's governor.

The court's chief justice was William Stoughton, a deeply religious man who believed in spectral evidence. Jonathan Corwin and John Hathorne were among the other judges as well. Some of the accused never even made it to trial. Sarah Osborne died in jail before being tried. So did three others.

A LACK OF JUSTICE

When the trials began, the juries heard the evidence against the accused. They watched while the bewitched girls twitched, screamed, and pointed to those on trial. The judges did not even try to quiet them.

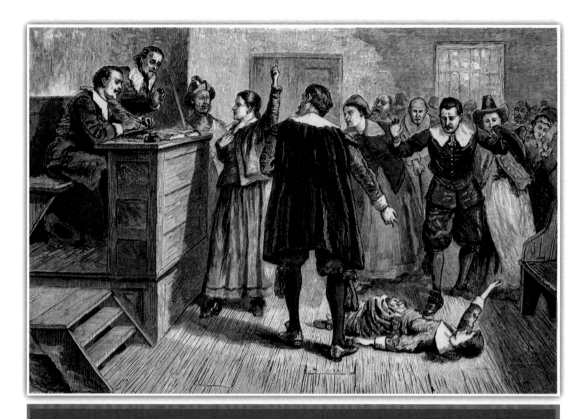

During the trials, the young accusers fell to the floor, twitching. They also imitated the movements of those on trial. This proved to many that the helpless defendants were guilty.

Sarah Good was found guilty and sentenced to hang. While in jail, she tried to kill herself three times. Then on July 19, she was taken outside and hanged. Before she was hanged, a minister spoke to Sarah Good. He told her to confess to save her soul. Good answered: "You're a liar! I am no more a witch than you are a wizard! If you take away my life, God will give you blood to drink." On the day Sarah Good was put to death, Rebecca Nurse and three others were hanged as well, and the executions continued.

A MISTAKE?

On August 19, five more people were hanged, including John Proctor and George Burroughs. Their bodies were dumped into a common grave. Burroughs had worn his best suit. Thieves removed it from his corpse after he was buried.

Just before dying, Burroughs said the Lord's Prayer perfectly. Since Puritans believed that a witch or wizard could not do this, Burrough's prayer made the crowd uneasy. They thought he might have been innocent. He was hanged anyway.

PRESSED TO DEATH

The hangings did not stop. Eight more people were executed on September 22. Among these were Mary Easty and Martha Corey.

Giles Corey, Martha Corey's husband, had been accused as well. When asked if he was a wizard, seventy-year-old Giles Corey refused to answer. He knew no one would believe he was innocent.

Corey was tortured to make him confess. Heavy stones were placed on his body, which killed him two days later. Despite the pain, Giles Corey did not confess.

Others were less brave. Many admitted to crimes they did not do. Those who confessed and repented, or said they were sorry, lived. The people who insisted they were innocent were hanged. That was how things were in Salem Village.

George Burroughs recited the Lord's Prayer before his hanging. This should have been a sign that Burroughs was not a wizard, but the reverend was executed just the same.

WHY DID IT HAPPEN?

T he Salem Witch trials finally ended when the last eight people were executed, on September 22. In all, twenty people had been killed. By that time, many people were tired of all the arrests and hangings. The bewitched young women had even accused some relatives of the judges. No one was going to put those people on trial.

THE GOVERNOR STEPS IN

On September 29, Massachusetts Governor Phips returned from a trip to find over one hundred people still in jail awaiting trial. Phips knew that things had gone too far. On October 8, he ordered that there be no further arrests or trials for witchcraft. The nightmare was finally over.

The trials had hurt Salem Village. They had taken up too much of the villagers' time and energy. Farms and business

Governor Phips had gone on a trip to Maine, expecting the trials and punishments to be completed before his return. Instead, he found a jail full of accused witches.

suffered. The jailings and executions left young children without parents. Bad feelings had deepened between the families and friends of the accused and their accusers.

NO CLEAR ANSWERS

No one can explain for certain what happened in Salem Village. The trouble may have started because some bored young women wanted attention. After that, much of Salem Village may have simply become caught up in the frenzy of a witch hunt. Or was there more to it?

Many of the accused were disliked by the large and powerful Putnam family. Young Ann Putnam accused quite a number of people. After a while, Ann's mother also appeared bewitched. She began accusing people of witchcraft as well. However, Ann's mother had a long history of mental problems.

Some historians feel that land may have had a lot to do with the trials. People found guilty of witchcraft lost all their property. Some of the accused owned plots of land that many villagers wanted. The other villagers were eager to buy these plots cheaply.

Another, less common, theory is that the bewitched girls might have had ergot poisoning. Ergot is a fungus that grows on grains. At the time of the witchcraft trials, rye was grown in the area and people in Salem Village ate rye bread. Ergot poisoning could have caused much of the behavior the girls displayed.

Still another reason for the witchcraft trials may be tied to the settlers' fears about the local Indians. During the 1670s and 1680s, fighting with the Wabanaki Indians took its toll on the settlers. Many on New England's frontier lost family members, homes,

Some experts believe that the villagers' fear of the local American Indians fueled their frenzy. The people of Salem easily believed any bad happenings were the work of the devil.

EXPLORE THE FACTS

APOLOGIES

After the trials, some jury members apologized. They knew that they had found innocent people guilty. The families of some of the victims received money for their losses, as well.

and livestock during attacks. The Puritans believed that the Indian attacks, like witchcraft, were caused by the devil. They were anxious to see an end to both. Therefore, it may not be surprising that the witchcraft trials took place.

CHAPTER EIGHT

THE LEGACY OF SALEM

Salem Village was never quite the same after the witchcraft trials and executions. Here is what happened to a few of the villagers.

Betty Parris, the girl who started the whole frenzy, was sent by her father to live with a close family friend. Out of Salem, Betty no longer felt bewitched. She later married and had five children.

In 1706, Ann Putnam publicly said she was sorry for her role in the Salem witchcraft trials. She never married, and she died when she was just thirty-seven years old.

As a five-year-old, Dorcas Good remained jailed for nearly eight months. After her release, she was no longer the healthy cheerful child she had been. She became quiet and sad and seemed to lose interest in life. Some say that she later went insane.

Tituba remained in jail nearly a year longer than the others arrested for witchcraft. Prisoners had to pay for their room and board while jailed. Reverend Parris would not pay Tituba's bill.

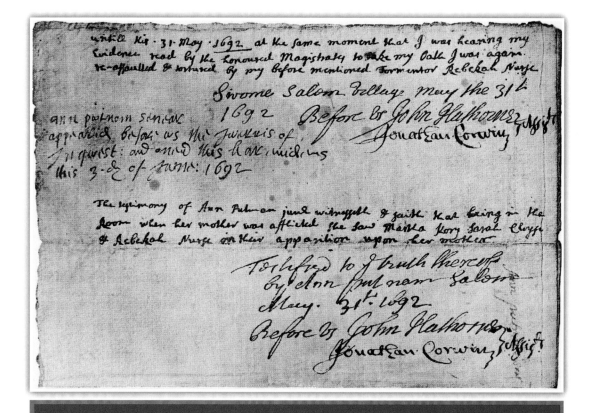

This document records the deposition given by Ann Putnam and her daughter. It may be shocking to Americans today that such flimsy testimony was enough to convict so many people.

Finally, someone bought Tituba from Parris and paid her debt. Though out of jail, she remained a slave.

Following the witchcraft trials, support for Reverend Parris lessened. He had not remained open-minded about those accused. Instead, Parris had given several sermons in which he preached against them. Rebecca Nurse's relatives were especially against him remaining reverend of the church. In 1697, Parris left Salem Village to become a minister in western

Massachusetts. In time, he left there, too. After that, he worked as a schoolteacher and merchant.

STILL RELEVANT TODAY

Salem Village does not exist today. That's because it became the town of Danvers, Massachusetts, in 1752. Danvers has many witchcraft museums. You can still visit Jonathan Corwin's

The Salem Village Witchcraft Memorial pays tribute to the victims of the witchcraft trials. The memorial is located in Danvers, Massachusetts, the current site of Salem Village.

Though not the actual site of the trials, Salem, Massachusetts, features a wax museum devoted to the notorious event. Visitors come from far and wide to learn about the nearly unbelievable events that transpired centuries ago.

Reverend Samuel Parris suffered a damaged reputation as a result of the witch trials. It didn't help that he took years to apologize for his behavior during a crisis he may have helped foster. For this and other reasons, his congregation lost faith in him. Parris left Salem Village in 1697. His departure allowed the townspeople to heal.

house or Rebecca Nurse's farm. A monument and small park in Danvers honors those who died because of the trials.

Hundreds of years later, some still wonder how those unfair trials could have happened. People have written books and plays about it. People often blame the bewitched young women for what happened. Yet the Salem Village adults are also to blame for taking them seriously. They arrested, tried, and hanged the accused.

Many important individuals in the area also did not do enough to stop it. They only spoke out once their family members were accused. Without a doubt, the blame for what happened in Salem Village must be shared.

Today, we have an entirely different justice system in America. According to the rules of this system, "justice" must always be fair and truly just. The Salem witchcraft trials are an important reminder of why that is important.

1691

Salem Village experiences a brutally cold winter.

1692

January—Betty Parris and Abigail Williams begin behaving strangely and are thought to be bewitched.

mid-February—A number of young women in Salem Village show signs of being bewitched.

February 29—Warrants for the arrest of Tituba, Sarah Good, and Sarah Osborne are issued.

March 1—Tituba, Sarah Good, and Sarah Osborne are questioned at the meetinghouse.

March 11—Martha Corey is accused of witchcraft.

March 21—Martha Corey is questioned at the meetinghouse.

March 28—Elizabeth Proctor is accused of witchcraft.

April 11—Elizabeth Proctor is questioned at the meetinghouse. John Proctor is accused of being a wizard.

May 4—George Burroughs is arrested for being a wizard and brought to Salem from Maine to be questioned.

mid-June—The actual trials begin.

July 19—Sarah Good, Rebecca Nurse, and others are executed for witchcraft.

August 19—Five more people are hanged, including John Proctor and George Burroughs.

September 19—Giles Corey is tortured to death. Heavy stones were placed on his body.

TIMELINE

September 22—Eight people are hanged, including Martha Corey and Mary Easty.

September 29—Governor Phips returns from a trip to Maine.

October 8—Governor Phips orders that there will be no further arrests or trials for witchcraft.

October 29—The court set up to handle the witchcraft cases is dissolved.

1697

Reverend Samuel Parris leaves Salem Village.

1703

A law is passed in Massachusetts forbidding the use of spectral evidence in trials.

1706

Ann Putnam apologizes for her role in the Salem witchcraft trials.

1752

Salem Village becomes the town of Danvers, Massachusetts.

BABBLE—To speak as if in a strange language.

BEWITCHED—Having had a spell cast on a person by a witch.

BLIZZARD—A large snowstorm.

EXECUTE—To take someone's life as punishment for a crime.

INSANE—Having problems with the way a person thinks or behaves.

MAGISTRATE—A judge.

PACT—An agreement.

REPENT—To be sorry for wrongdoing.

SPECTRAL EVIDENCE—A statement in court that a person's spirit left his or her body and harmed others.

TORTURE—To cause a person great physical pain.

WITCHCRAFT—Black or evil magic.

WIZARD—A male thought to have magic powers.

FURTHER READING

Benoit, Peter. *The Salem Witch Trials.* New York: Children's Press, 2014.

Doeden, Matt. *The Salem Witch Trials: An Interactive History Adventure.* Mankato, MN: Capstone Press, 2011.

Fremon, David K. *The Salem Witchcraft Trials in United States History.* Berkeley Heights, NJ: Enslow Publishers, 2015.

Holub, Joan and Dede Putra. *What Were the Salem Witch Trials?* New York: Grosset & Dunlap, 2015.

Marciniak, Kristin. *The Salem Witch Trials.* Ann Arbor, MI: Cherry Lake Publishing, 2014.

Martin, Michael. *The Salem Witch Trials.* Oxford, England: Raintree, 2012.

Smith, Andrea P. *The Salem Witch Trials.* New York: PowerKids Press, 2012.

Stewart, Gail B. *The Salem Witch Trials.* San Diego, CA: ReferencePoint Press, 2013.

FOR MORE INFORMATION

NATIONAL GEOGRAPHIC: SALEM WITCH-HUNT-INTERACTIVE

www.nationalgeographic.com/salem

Experience what it was like to be accused of witchcraft during the 1692 Salem witchcraft trials in this exciting online trial.

SALEM WAX MUSEUM

www.salemwaxmuseum.com

Experience the terror of the Salem Witch Trials of 1692, but do not miss the link marked "Education" on this fascinating website.

SALEM WITCH MUSEUM

www.salemwitchmuseum.com

Visit this website to see what it was like to be a Salem Villager in 1692. This website has some wonderful pictures.

INDEX